SPORTS MATH MANIA!

COOL STATS AND NUMBER FACTS

By Lorraine Jean Hopping
and Christopher Egan

A SPORTS ILLUSTRATED FOR KIDS BOOK

Sports Math Mania!
A SPORTS ILLUSTRATED FOR KIDS Book/October 1996

SPORTS ILLUSTRATED FOR KIDS and KiDS are registered trademarks of Time Inc.

Cover and interior design by Miriam Dustin
Cover and interior illustrations by Mick McGinty

For information, address: SPORTS ILLUSTRATED FOR KIDS

Sports Math Mania! is published by SPORTS ILLUSTRATED FOR KIDS, a division of Time Inc. Its trademark is registered in the U.S. Patent and Trademark Office and in other countries. SPORTS ILLUSTRATED FOR KIDS, 1271 Avenue of the Americas, New York, NY 10020

PRINTED IN THE UNITED STATES OF AMERICA
10 9 8 7 6 5 4 3 2 1

ISBN 1-886749-18-3

Sports Math Mania! is a production of SPORTS ILLUSTRATED FOR KIDS Books: Cathrine Wolf, Editorial Director; Margaret Sieck, Senior Editor; Jill Safro, Stephen Thomas, Associate Editors (Project Editors), Sherie Holder, Assistant Editor

TABLE OF CONTENTS

INTRODUCTION

What can you do in $\frac{1}{100}$ of a second? Not much! But that's how long a batter has to connect with a blazing fastball. The swing has to be timed just right or . . . *WHIFF!*

Timing is important in sports. So are speed, strength, and concentration. Without them, you'd be in trouble on most playing fields. The same goes for math.

Without math, sports would not exist! Don't believe us? Try to describe an exciting game without using any numbers. We bet you can't do it. Why? Numbers are important sports "equipment," just like bats, balls, hoops, and hurdles.

Can you tell a good sports number from a bad one? Can you figure Michael Jordan's points-per-game average? Can you decide who's the better player: Ken Griffey, Senior, or Ken Griffey, Junior? Once you've read *Sports Math Mania!*, you'll be able to do all these things and more.

Sports Math Mania! will give you the inside scoop on all the major sports stats. It will help you sort the legends from the losers. And it will dazzle your brain with cool sports trivia and wacky facts.

Are you hungry for super stats and major league math? *Sports Math Mania!* has your number!

CHAPTER 1

BASEBALL

Flip to the back of a baseball card. What do you see? Numbers. Lots of numbers. If you're a baseball fan, chances are you are a number fan, too. After all, what would baseball be without numbers?

The back of a 1996 Albert Belle card lists these numbers: 173 hits, 121 runs, 52 doubles, 50 home runs, 126 runs batted in (RBIs). Are these good stats for a major leaguer? For one season, they're outstanding. But for a long-time veteran, it could mean it's time to retire.

What's the best way to compare baseball totals? With averages.

WHAT'S A BATTING AVERAGE?

Average can mean common, ordinary, or even dull. But stick the word *batting* in front of it and *average* can mean exciting, talented, or even superstar. Why? Because batting averages let us judge how good a hitter is at the plate.

A batting average is a ratio. It compares the number of hits a player gets to the number of chances he had.

Say you are batting for the Baltimore Orioles. You step up to the plate for the 60th time this season. Here

RONALD C. MODRA/SPORTS ILLUSTRATED

CAL RIPKEN, JUNIOR

comes the pitch . . . home run! It's your 20th hit of the year. What's your batting average? To find out, divide the number of hits by the number of at-bats:

20 hits ÷ 60 at-bats = .300

The answer is another way of writing 30 percent. It's the same as 30 out of 100, or $\frac{30}{100}$. If you reduce the fraction, you get $\frac{3}{10}$. That means you hit safely in 3 out of every 10 at-bats! Here's an example of a weaker average:

50 hits ÷ 250 at-bats = .200

A .200 average is 20% or 2 hits out of every 10 at-bats. With 3 hits out of 10 at-bats, the batting average jumps to an impressive .300.

Here are some players' real stats. Figure out their batting averages, and learn who's the best of the bunch.

	Hits	At-bats	Average
Albert Belle	173	546	_____
Chili Davis	135	424	_____
Edgar Martinez	182	511	_____

(Answers on pages 62–64)

ERA: PITCHERS GIVE IT UP

When a hitter steps up to the plate, he wants his batting average to go up. But the pitcher wants to *lower* an average of his own — his ERA. Earned run average (ERA) is the average number of runs a pitcher gives up over nine innings.

ERA pits all earned-run numbers against the same nine-inning scale, no matter how many innings a pitcher has pitched.

"Earned runs" are the runs that the pitcher is responsible for. They are his "fault." (Usually, runs that score because of errors are "unearned." They don't count against the pitcher.) Pitchers don't want to earn runs. When they do, their ERA goes up.

Say Dwight Gooden pitches on Opening Day. The New York Yankee ace allows three earned runs in nine innings. His ERA is:

$$9 \div 3 = 3.00 \text{ ERA}$$

WACKY FACTS

o A fastball travels from the pitcher's mound to home plate faster than you can say "baseball." The time it spends over home plate is $\frac{1}{100}$ of a second.

o In a three-hour baseball game, the ball is in play for about 10 minutes!

What if Dwight allows five earned runs over the next 12 innings he pitches? Has his ERA gone up or down? Here's how to find out:

Figure the total number of runs Dwight has allowed so far in the season (8). Multiply that total by 9 (because ERA is based on a nine-inning scale):

$$8 \times 9 = 72$$

Now, divide 72 by the number of innings, Dwight has pitched this year (21):

$$72 \div 21 = 3.43 \text{ ERA}$$

An ERA of 3.43 is good, but not great. But what if Dwight allows just seven earned runs in the next 30 innings? What's his new ERA? HINT: *The new totals are 15 runs and 51 innings pitched.*   (*Answer on pages 62–64*)

BY THE NUMBERS

Can you identify the "iron" Oriole by his numbers?

BIRTH DATE: 8/24/60

JERSEY NUMBER: 8

CLAIM TO FAME:
More than 2,131 consecutive games played

FAMOUS DATE: 9/6/95

(Answer on pages 62–64)

WACKY FACT

Is 3 a lucky number? A turn-of-the-century pitcher named Rube Waddell probably thought so. He once struck out three batters with three pitches apiece in the third inning. Not bad for a player who was born on a Friday the 13th!

NOBODY'S PERFECT

Percentages come up a lot in baseball. Here is a list of some basic ones:

.100	1 out of 10
.200	1 out of 5
.250	1 out of 4
.333	1 out of 3
.500	1 out of 2
.750	3 out of 4
1.000	10 out of 10 (perfect)

THE GOOD, THE BAD, AND THE AVERAGE

POOF! We've turned you into a baseball scout. Now take a look at the following stats:

1. Runs Batted In (RBIs): When you get a hit, a walk, or make an out and a runner scores, you get one RBI. If two runners score, you get two RBIs. If *three* runners score . . . well, you get the idea.

If a batter gets 9 RBIs in a season, did he have a good year or a bad year? How about 9 RBIs in a game?

2. Win-Loss Percentage: If you win half your games, you've won 50 percent of them. Of course, you've lost 50 percent of them, too. In baseball, 50 percent is written .500. Anything above .500 is a winning record.

Say a team finishes a season with a win-loss percentage of .590 — is that good, bad, or so-so?

(Answers on pages 62–64)

THINK FAST!

Why did a minor leaguer named John Neves wear a backward 7 on his uniform?   *(Answer on pages 62–64)*

ABOVE AVERAGE

Boston Red Sox legend Ted Williams once had an amazing batting average. It was so high that no one has equaled it for more than 50 years.

In 1941, Ted had 456 at-bats. His hit total was 185! What was Ted's awesome average for the season?

(Answer on pages 62–64)

MICHAEL ZITO/SPORTSCHROME EAST/WEST

GREG MADDUX

BELOW AVERAGE

The best batting average in the league is usually in the high .300's. In 1923 and 1926, Babe Ruth cranked out averages of .393 and .372. Yet he still did not win the American League batting title.

In 1968, Carl Yastrzemski of the Boston Red Sox won the

BY THE NUMBERS

Can you identify
this star player by his numbers?
BIRTH DATE: 11/25/14
JERSEY NUMBER: 5
POSITION: Centerfielder
HEIGHT: 6 feet 2 inches
CLAIM TO FAME: Hit in 56 consecutive games
FAMOUS YEAR: 1941

(Answer on
pages 62–64)

title with the lowest average ever. He had 162 hits in 539 at-bats. What was his average?   *(Answer on pages 62–64)*

MYSTERY PITCHER

Only one pitcher has won the Cy Young award four times in a row. In his fourth award-winning year, the pitcher had 38 earned runs in 209 innings pitched. What was his ERA? When you figure it out, you'll know which of these pitchers is the "mystery pitcher."   *(Answer on pages 62–64)*

Roger Clemens	1.93
Bob Gibson	1.12
Tom Glavine	3.08
Randy Johnson	2.48
Greg Maddux	1.63
Mike Mussina	3.29
Hideo Nomo	2.54
Cy Young	1.62

LITTLE LEAGUE CHAMPS

There's no doubt about it. When it comes to big-league baseball, the United States rules. But what about *Little League* baseball? How do our younger players stack up against world competition?

This graph shows who has won the Little League World Series since 1970. After you've looked it over, you'll know who's tops in Little League. How many championships has that team won? *(Answers on pages 62–64)*

NUMBER HALL OF FAME

The numbers below are baseball's most famous all-time records. They're so famous that you can probably identify the records just by looking at the numbers.

(Answers on pages 62–64)

A.	755	1.	RBIs in a season
B.	61	2.	Career RBIs
C.	4,256	3.	Career victories for a pitcher
D.	56	4.	Home runs in a season
E.	511	5.	Career base hits
F.	190	6.	Career home runs
G.	2,297	7.	Career strikeouts for a pitcher
H.	5,714	8.	Games in a row with a base hit

WELCOME TO THE CLUB?

Only six major leaguers have hit 400 home runs and 3,000 hits in a career. Was Al Kaline one of them? In 22 years, the Detroit Tiger outfielder averaged about 18 home runs and 137 hits per year. Is that enough for Al to join the 400–3,000 club? *(Answer on pages 62–64)*

WHERE THE SON SHINES

Ken Griffey, Junior, Barry Bonds, and Moises Alou have major league shoes to fill. Their dads played baseball for years, racking up fantastic stats. The sons haven't played as long. Yet, in some areas, they've already passed their pops. Use the table on page 16 to answer these questions:

1. In which stat could the sons *pass* their fathers but fall behind again?

2. Who is a better power hitter (more extra-base hits) — Ken Griffey, Senior, or Ken Griffey, Junior?

3. Of the three dads, who do you think was the best player? Why do you think so?

4. Who is the best of the sons? Why?

5. What is the only fair way to compare players who have played different amounts of time?

(Answers on pages 62–64)

STATS*

	At-bats	Hits	Avg.	HR	2B	3B	RBI
Ken Griffey, Sr.	7,229	2,143	.296	152	364	77	859
Ken Griffey, Jr.	3,440	1,039	.302	189	201	19	585
Bobby Bonds	7,043	1,886	.268	332	302	66	1024
Barry Bonds	5,020	1,436	.286	292	306	48	864
Felipe Alou	7,339	2,101	.286	206	359	49	852
Moises Alou	1,609	475	.295	63	110	14	277

Statistics are through the 1995 season. (Avg. is short for average; HR stands for home run; 2B is short for double; 3B means triple; RBI is an abbreviation of runs batted in)

WACKY FACT

The first team to wear numbers on its uniforms was the New York Yankees, in 1929. Starting players wore numbers that matched their usual places in the batting order. That's why Babe Ruth wore number 3 — he batted third!

CHAPTER 2

BASKETBALL

In baseball, only the best major league hitters get a hit in three out of every 10 at-bats (a .300 average). There's a flip side to this stand-out stat: The world's best players fail 7 out of 10 times they bat.

If an NBA player missed 7 out of every 10 free throws, he'd find himself sitting on the bench in a hurry. And if he only made only 1 out of every 10 shots? He'd be looking for a new job!

Good numbers in one sport can be a disaster in another. In fact, good numbers in one *game* can be a disaster in another game. Read on and learn how.

SCORING BIG AND BIG SCORING

In 1990, the Denver Nuggets scored 158 points against the Golden State Warriors in a National Basketball Association (NBA) game. Big win, right? Wrong! The Nuggets lost by 4 points! Final score: Warriors 162, Nuggets 158. The teams set an NBA record for highest combined score without overtime.

As you can see, numbers by themselves don't mean much. To understand the numbers, you must compare them to other numbers.

Comparing game scores is easy. The larger number wins. Comparing totals is just as simple.

In college, Sheryl Swoopes once scored 47 points. If that were a season total, no one would have ever heard of Sheryl. But she scored a record 47 points in the finals of the 1993 National Collegiate Athletic Association (NCAA) tournament. That makes Sheryl's 47 an excellent total in any book!

BE LIKE MIKE

For most NBA players, scoring 20 points a game is great. For Chicago Bulls superstar Michael "Air" Jordan, anything under 30 points is so-so. How do we know? Because in his 11-year career, Michael has averaged an amazing 32 points per game.

In seven straight seasons, between 1986–87 and 1992–93, Michael led the NBA in scoring. He also led the league in scoring for the eighth time in 1995–1996.

WACKY FACT

One of the worst basketball teams in Olympic history was the 1948 squad from Iraq. The Iraqis gave up an average of 104 points per game. Against Korea and China, Iraq lost by a margin of 100 points! Even worse, they averaged only 23.5 points per game.

Believe it or not, at the same Olympics, there was another team that scored even fewer points than the Iraqis. The Irish team averaged only 17 points per game!

No one has won more scoring titles than Mike. To figure his scoring average for 1986–87, divide the total points (Pts) by the number of games played (Gm). Then round to one decimal place:

3,041 ÷ 82 = 37.085

MICHAEL JORDAN

The stats for Michael's top-scoring years are listed below. First, fill in the missing averages. Then tell us: In which season did Michael have the highest average? *(Answers on pages 62-64)*

	Gm	Pts	Avg
1986–87	82	3,041	____
1987–88	82	2,868	____
1988–89	81	2,633	____
1989–90	82	2,753	33.6
1990–91	82	2,580	____
1991–92	80	2,404	30.1
1992–93	78	2,541	32.6

Other per-game averages work the same way. For example, divide the number of rebounds by the number of games played. Do the same to figure a player's average for assists, steals, and blocked shots.

POINTS ON A PLATTER

If someone handed you the ball and gave you a free shot at the basket, you'd probably take it. But would you make it? Free throws, or the shots a player takes when he's been fouled, seem like an easy way to score. But sometimes even the greatest players can't hit a thing when they're given a free shot.

During his 14-year career, Wilt Chamberlain hit an incredible 54% of his shots. But what was his free throw average? Did he make more free throws than he missed?

To find out, look at Wilt's career stats: 6,057 hits out of 11,862 attempts. Then divide the number of free-throws-made by the number of attempts:

6,057 (shots made) ÷ 11,682 (attempts) = .51062

Next, round to three places to the right of the decimal: .511. Wilt's free throw percentage was .511. A percentage of .500 means 50 out of 100 — or half. So any

BY THE NUMBERS

Can you identify
this eight-time NBA scoring leader?
BIRTH DATE: 2/17/63
JERSEY NUMBERS: 23, 45
HEIGHT: 6 feet, 6 inches
CLAIM TO FAME:
an average of 33.9 points per playoff game
FAMOUS FEAT: "3-peat"

WACKY FACT

Is it possible to catch a ball, turn, and shoot in one tenth of a second? In 1990, Trent Tucker of the New York Knicks caught and launched a game-winning basket with .1 second on the game clock. The problem is, scientists say that no human can shoot that fast. The shot probably took half a second. The referee and the scorer took too much time before they started the game clock. What do you think? If you played in "Trent Tucker time," you could shoot 100 shots in 10 seconds!

percentage under .500 means more misses than hits. Wilt just made it over .500.

In 1980–81, Calvin Murphy of the Houston Rockets barely missed at all! Calvin made 206 of 215 foul shots and set an NBA record with a percentage of .958.

There are other percentages in basketball. They are:

Win-Loss: To figure a team's winning percentage, divide the number of games won by the number of games played. For example, 41 wins ÷ 82 games played = .500.

Field Goals: Divide the number of shots from the field made by the number attempted. In most cases, field goal percentages are lower than free throw percentages.

3-Point Field Goals: Same as above, but only for 3-point shots.

WELL-SEASONED

Anyone can have a bad game. Anyone can have a good game, too. That's the great thing about averages — the bad and the good "average out" over a long season.

To figure a player's *career* average, first add the totals for every game in the player's career. For example, Moses Malone scored 27,409 points during his 19-year career. He played in 1,329 games. To figure his average, divide:

27,409 (points) ÷ 1,329 (games played) = 20.6 points per game

Moses stacked up the points, but lots of players have scored more points *per game* than Moses. The difference is that Moses played a lot of games. Players who score more points in fewer games will have a higher average per game.

TRIPLE DOUBLE TIME

A "triple double" is like a hat trick in hockey (3 goals by one player). It means that in one game, a player racks up double digit statistics (10 or more) in three categories. Usually, the categories are points, rebounds, and assists.

WACKY FACT

Who holds the record for making the most free throws? Not an NBA star. According to the Guinness Book of Records, on November 15, 1993, Thomas Amberry sank 2,750 free throws in a row!

BY THE NUMBERS

Can you identify
this retired Los Angeles Laker
by his numbers?

BIRTH DATE: 4/16/47
JERSEY NUMBER: 33
HEIGHT: 7 feet, 2 inches
CLAIM TO FAME: The Skyhook

In 1961–62, Oscar Robertson, who played for the Cincinnati Royals, averaged 30.8 points, 11.4 assists, and 12.5 rebounds per game — for the entire season!

SHORTCUTS

There's a lot to remember in the world of hoops, but these abbreviations should make things a bit easier:

AST = assists
ATT = attempts
FG = field goal (shot other than a free throw)
FT = free throw
PF = personal foul
PCT = percentage
PTS = points
REB = rebounds

GIVE THEM A HAND

John Stockton of the Utah Jazz and Magic Johnson, formerly of the Los Angeles Lakers, rank first and second in all-time NBA assists. So who would you rather have in your back court? It's a close call. Figure their assists-per-game averages and decide.

John Stockton: 980 games, 11,310 assists

Magic Johnson: 906 games, 10,141 assists

RODMAN'S REBOUNDS

In 1995–96, Dennis Rodman became the second NBA player ever to win the rebounding championship five times in a row. Between the 1991–92 and 1995–96 seasons, Dennis grabbed 5,809 rebounds in 306 games. What was Dennis's per-game average?

(Answers on pages 62-64)

FOUL CALL

Imagine you're the coach of the next Olympic Dream Team. Late in the gold-medal game, the score is tied when a technical foul is called on a player from the other team. You may choose one of your players on the court to shoot the free throw. Here are the career free-throw stats for three Dream Team veterans. Figure their career free-throw percentage to see who's your best bet:

1. Reggie Miller: 3,616 shots made out of 4,122 attempts

2. Shaquille O'Neal: 1,602 shots made out of 2,936 attempts

3. Scottie Pippen: 2,106 shots made out of 3,065 attempts

BIG MEN ON COURT

Forget points, rebounds, and free throws for a minute. Basketball players post impressive numbers in another area — height!

Of course, all big stars start out small. But some start out smaller than others!

Have you ever wondered how tall Shaq was as a kid? How about David Robinson? Read the chart below to see how some NBA giants measured up over the years.

	Shawn Bradley	Shaquille O'Neal	David Robinson	Wilt Chamberlain
Age 10	6' 0"	5' 3"	5' 0"	6' 3"
Age 14	6' 8"	6' 8"	5' 9"	7' 0"
Age 18	7' 5"	7' 1"	6' 7"	7' 0"
Adult	7' 6"	7' 1"	7' 1"	7' 1"

THE 25,000 POINT CLUB

Only 12 players have scored at least 25,000 points in their careers. Some scored their points in the NBA and the American Basketball Association (ABA) combined, while others reached the mark only in the NBA. Either way, it's an impressive accomplishment.

1. Kareem Abdul-Jabbar (38,387 points)
2. Wilt Chamberlain (31,419 points)
3. Julius Erving (30,026 points)
4. Dan Issel (27,482 points)
5. Moses Malone (27,360 points)
6. Elvin Hayes (27,313 points)
7. Oscar Robertson (26,710 points)
8. George Gervin (26,595 points)
9. John Havlicek (26,395 points)
10. Alex English (25,613 points)
11. Rick Barry (25,279 points)
12. Jerry West (25,192 points)

DAVID ROBINSON

WACKY FACT

It isn't easy being as tall as the 7' 1" David Robinson. When David gets into cars, his knees squish against the steering wheel. When he takes a shower, the water hits him in the stomach!

RICH KANE/SPORTS ILLUSTRATED

CHAPTER 3

SOCCER

Every January, about 140 million Americans watch the Super Bowl on TV. That's a lot of people. But every four years about two *billion* people watch soccer's World Cup finals. Now *that* is a lot of people!

There are roughly six billion people in the world. That means about one out of every three Earthlings tunes in to the same game at the same time. It also means that soccer is the *numero-uno* sport in the world. It's number one!

RANK PROFESSIONALS

Soccer may be the number-one sport, but which country has the number-one team? Soccer teams from around the world play for regional championships in North America, South America, Central America, Europe, Africa, and Asia. FIFA is the international organization that runs soccer. It ranks teams based on points.

Winning is an excellent way to score points. Another sure-fire point-getter is to play tough teams. The third way is to avoid small tournaments. Only big "important" tournaments help a team's score. (FIFA decides what is important.) The final factor is to score a lot of goals — without letting other teams score many against you.

Every year, countries are ranked by their point totals. Countries that have competed in the World Cup also have an all-time ranking. Here are the top five teams in World Cup competition:

Team	Points
1. Brazil	111
2. Germany	100
3. Italy	84
4. Argentina	61
5. England	48

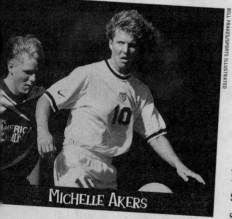

MICHELLE AKERS

In case you are wondering, the United States is ranked 29th, with 9 points.

35 COUNTRIES CAN'T BE WRONG

Only men play in the World Cup. But soccer is a hugely popular women's sport, too. In fact, women's soccer is so popular that it is now an official Olympic sport. How does a women's sport make it into the Olympics? It must be played in at least 35 different countries.

By 1996, women's soccer had hit that magic number. Led by superstars Michelle Akers and Mia Hamm,

Team USA joined nations from around the world in the first women's Olympic soccer competition!

HEADS UP!

To understand the numbers in soccer, you have to get a grip on the letters. Here are some of the common abbreviations used in the game:

A = assists
G = goals
GA = goals against (what others scored against you)
GF = goals for (what you scored)
Pts = points (3 for a win; 1 for a tie)
W–L–T = games won, lost, tied

KIDS COUNT

How many kids play soccer around the world? One million? Two million? Try 200 million! About 12 million play right here in the United States. That makes soccer the number three sport with American kids. Only basketball and volleyball are more popular.

POWERFUL PELÉ

Pelé was greatest player in soccer history. The Brazilian superstar played for 20 years. He scored 1,282 goals in 1,355 games! What was his goals per game average? To find out, divide. Then round your answer to two decimal places.

$$1,282 \text{ goals} \div 1,355 \text{ games} = ?$$

(Answer on pages 62–64)

GOAL-FOR-IT

In the championship match of the 1994 World Cup, Brazil and Italy were tied 0–0 after 120 minutes of play. What happens when there is a tie in a Final? A shootout! (Teams alternate penalty shots.) Brazil won, 3–2.

Never before had regulation time run out in a Final without a goal being scored. The graph below shows the average goals per World Cup match since the tournament began in 1930. (There was no World Cup competition between 1938 and 1950 because of World War II.)

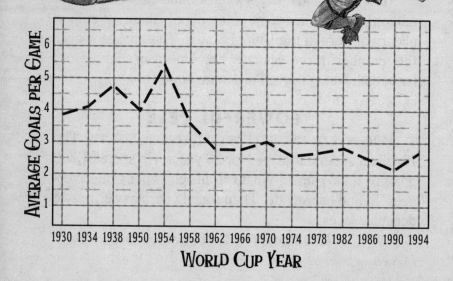

WORLD CUP YEAR

CHAPTER 4

FOOTBALL

What does every football player struggle for? What are these guys grunting and sweating and knocking heads over? Yards. It's that simple. Passing yards. Running yards. Kicking yards. Return yards. Punting yards. Yards, yards, yards! Without yards, there aren't too many touchdowns or field goals. And if no one scores, no one wins.

WIN SOME, LOSE SOME

One team's gain is another team's loss. Detroit Lion running back Barry Sanders picks up 34 yards. Does the crowd cheer? Only if the game is in Detroit. The opposing team has just given up 34 yards.

On the next play, Barry is tackled behind the line of scrimmage. It's a loss of four yards for Detroit. What's Barry's *net gain* so far? This term may sound like high finance, but it's pure football. Barry gained 34 yards and lost 4 yards. So, subtract the loss from the gain: 34 − 4. The net gain is 30 yards.

Barry will definitely run again. And again and again. By the end of the game, he'll have lots of gains and probably a few losses, too. Subtract the losses from the gains, and Barry might wind up with a net gain of 150 yards.

If Barry does gain 150 yards, that means he'll score a lot of points, right? Not necessarily. The yards aren't worth much unless Barry gains them near the other team's goal line. William "Refrigerator" Perry of the Chicago Bears gained just 11 yards in 1985. But, most of The Fridge's rushing attempts and catches came near the opponent's end zone. The Fridge scored three touchdowns, or 18 points!

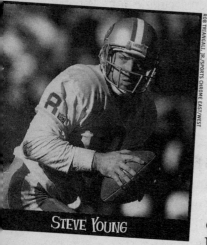

ROB TRIANGALI, JR./SPORTS CHROME EAST/WEST

STEVE YOUNG

AIRBORNE DIVISION

Suppose quarterback Brett Favre of the Green Bay Packers throws the football one yard. Wide receiver Robert Brooks catches it. The pass is complete. Robert runs 89 yards down the field. Brett is credited with a one-yard pass, and Robert receives credit for 89 yards rushing, right? Nope. Even though only one yard was gained in the air, Brett is credited with a 90-yard pass, and Robert is credited with a 90-yard catch.

In 11 NFL seasons, San Francisco 49er quarterback Steve Young has gained 23,069 passing yards. That's more than 13 miles (23,069 yards divided by 1,760 yards per mile). Sounds pretty great. But is it?

If Steve threw millions of passes, that stat would be weak. But he gained all those yards in only 2,876 pass attempts. (Incomplete passes gain zero yards.) To rank

Steve's stat on a list of all-star quarterbacks, you have to find the average number of yards per pass attempt:

**23,069 yards ÷ 2,876 pass attempts =
8.02 yards per pass attempt**

PASS-ABILITY

Quarterbacks get credit (or blame) for the result of every pass they throw. Passes are either caught (complete), dropped (incomplete), or intercepted. During his career, Steve Young has completed 1,845 of his 2,876 attempts. Finding the percentage is like figuring a batting average. Divide as follows:

1,845 ÷ 2,876 = 64.2 percent

That means that Steve has completed more than six of every 10 passes attempted. In baseball, a .642 batting average would be out of this world.

The last passing stat for quarterbacks is the

WACKY FACT

Jim Kelly of the Buffalo Bills is a great quarterback. During his 10-year NFL career, he has completed 2,652 passes for 32,657 yards and 223 touchdowns. But Jim has one number that won't "bowl" you over. He's the only quarterback to lose four straight Super Bowls. Jim and the Bills lost each Super Bowl from 1991 through 1994.

all-important one: touchdowns. In his career, Steve has thrown for 160 touchdowns and rushed for 30 more.

Statistics can help determine who is the greatest quarterback of them all. By combining a quarterback's stats, we can figure out his "quarterback rating." Here are a few of the statistics considered: completion and touchdown percentages, and average yards per attempt.

TOUCHDOWN!

Every once in a while, a quarterback gets to score a touchdown of his own. But usually, it's the receivers and running backs who get most of the glory. San Francisco 49er wide receiver Jerry Rice has scored the most touchdowns in NFL history: 155!

In 1987, Jerry Rice caught a record 22 touchdown passes in 12 games. That's almost two TD's per game:

22 touchdowns ÷ 12 games = 1.83 touchdowns per game

WACKY FACT

George Blanda, a quarterback and kicker, played in all or parts of four decades: the 1940s, '50s, '60s, and '70s. George's 26-year career was the longest in pro football history. No wonder he scored more points than anyone else (2,002). He also had more passes intercepted than anyone else (277)!

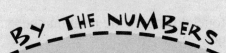

BY THE NUMBERS

Using his numbers as clues,
can you identify this Hall-of-Fame player?

BIRTH DATE: 7/25/54

JERSEY NUMBER: 34

POSITION: Running Back

HEIGHT: 5 feet, 10 inches

WEIGHT: 203 pounds

CLAIM TO FAME: This Chicago Bear is
professional football's all-time
leading rusher.

(Answer on
pages 62–64)

Emmitt Smith holds the record for rushing touchdowns in a season. In 1995, the Dallas Cowboy running back scored 25 touchdowns. He accomplished that over a 16-game season.

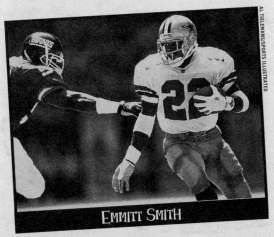

AL TIELEMANS/SPORTS ILLUSTRATED

EMMITT SMITH

Emmitt's 1995 touchdown per game average is excellent. But is it better than Jerry Rice's best average for 12 games?

To figure it out, divide Emmitt's total

number of touchdowns by the total number of games he played in 1995:

$$25 \text{ TDs} \div 16 \text{ games} = \underline{\hspace{2cm}}$$

(Answer on pages 62–64)

1 POINT AT A TIME

Who are the NFL's all-time scoring leaders? Believe it or not, the top scorers are *kickers!* But unlike running backs or quarterbacks, who score 6 points at a time, kickers score points more slowly — 3 points for a field goal and 1 for the point after a touchdown.

Kicking is like free throw shooting in basketball: Players want to be perfect. In 1981–82 Chuck Nelson of the University of Washington *was* perfect. He kicked 30 straight field goals! It was an NCAA-record.

Tony Zendejas of the Los Angeles Rams ended the 1991 season with a perfect record on field goal attempts.

BY THE NUMBERS

Can you identify
this star player by his numbers?
BIRTH DATE: 11/21/66
JERSEY NUMBER: 8
POSITION: Quarterback
CLAIM TO FAME: This Dallas Cowboy led his team to three Super Bowl wins before he reached the age of 30.

(Answer on
pages 62–64)

Tony made all 17 of the field goals he attempted! Most kickers are happy when they are successful 80 percent of the time.

SHORTCUTS

When you visit a new place, it helps to speak the local language. The same goes for football. When you are figuring football stats, it helps to know what these abbreviations stand for:

Att = Attempts
Cmp = Completions
FG = Field goals
PAT = Point after touchdowns
Pct = Percentage
Pts = Points
Rec = Receptions
TDs = Touchdowns
Yds = Yards

MILESTONES

Here's a list of the quarterbacks who have thrown for the greatest total distance (through the 1995 season):

Quarterback	Career Passing
Dan Marino	48,841 yards (about 28 miles)
Fran Tarkenton	47,003 yards (about 27 miles)
John Elway	41,706 yards (about 24 miles)
Joe Montana	40,551 yards (about 23 miles)

ANY WHICH WAY IT'S 12

There are many ways for a team to score 12 points in a game. Two 6-point touchdowns is one way to do it. Can you think of other ways? Use different combinations of field goals (3 points), safeties (2 points), and extra points or conversions (1 or 2 points after a touchdown) to figure it out.   *(Answer on pages 62–64)*

JUST PASSING BY

Quarterback Dan Marino holds the record for number of passing touchdowns in a season: 48 in 1984. There were 16 games in the season. How many touchdowns did Dan pass for *per game?*   *(Answer on pages 62–64)*

WHAT'S THE CATCH?

In 1994, Minnesota Viking Cris Carter caught 122 passes. It was a National Football League (NFL) record. Cris played in all 16 games that year. How many catches did he make *per game?*   *(Answer on pages 62–64)*

JIM VERSUS WALTER

Running back Jim Brown played nine seasons for the Cleveland Browns. Between 1957 and 1965, Jim gained a whopping 12,312 yards. Walter Payton, who played for the Chicago Bears from 1975 to 1987, racked up an all-time record of 16,726 yards.

Say Jim continued to gain 1,368 yards per year. If Jim played four more years (as long as Walter played), who would hold the record for the most yards gained?

(Answer on pages 62–64)

ALMOST PERFECT

Field-goal kickers can be perfect for a few kicks or a few games. Maybe, if they're really lucky, they can even be perfect for an entire season. But they certainly can't be perfect forever!

The career accuracy record is 366 field goals out of 455 attempts. Nick Lowery of the Kansas City Chiefs and the New York Jets gathered these stats from 1978 to 1995. What is his career percentage? *(Answer on pages 62–64)*

JUNIOR SEAU

RICH KANE/SPORTS CHROME EAST/WEST

TACKLING TERROR

San Diego Charger linebacker Junior Seau (pronounced *SAY-ow*) gives San Diego's defense a real jolt. Junior has led the Chargers in tackles five times. In his six-year career, Junior has totaled 729 tackles. How many tackles has he averaged per year? To find out, divide the number of tackles by the number of years:

729 tackles ÷ 6 years = ?

(Answer on pages 62–64)

OH, BROTHER!

Two pairs of brothers finished the 1994 season with pretty good numbers. The Sharpes (Sterling and

Shannon) and the Ismails (Raghib and Qadry, whose names are pronounced *RA-heeb* and *CAH-dree*) are all receivers. But who's the best brother team?

Check out their stats. The Sharpes have more receptions, more yards, and, in Sterling's case, more touchdowns. But the best player is the one who has the best average. That's the number of yards per reception. Figure each player's average. Then decide which brothers you'd rather have on your team!

	Rec	Yds	Avg	TD's
Sterling Sharpe	94	1,119	_____	18
Shannon Sharpe	87	1,010	_____	4
Raghib Ismail	34	513	_____	5
Qadry Ismail	45	696	_____	5

(Answer on pages 62–64)

CHAPTER 5

SWIMMING AND DIVING

One second is a short time for most people. But not if you're a diver! A champion diver can do three and a half somersaults in less than one second.

A second can be a long time for swimmers, too. In the 50-meter freestyle, it can mean the difference between a gold medal and a last-place finish.

Swimmers often win races by *fractions* of a second. That's why many swimmers try to make their bodies smooth for races. They wear skintight swimsuits and swim caps, and they shave all the hair off their bodies. Why? So there will be less resistance between their skin and the water. Resistance slows them down. Every fraction of a second counts.

A swimmer can win a race by ⅒ of a second (0.1). Another may squeak by the competition by 1/100 of a second (.01). Without electronic sensors, we wouldn't know who won! Will scorers ever need to use thousandths of a second (.001) to pick a winner? Only *time* will tell.

JANET EVANS

JUST A MINUTE

An Olympic pool is 50 meters long (about 164 feet). That is about the same distance as from the goal line to the opponent's 45-yard line on a football field. A top swimmer could cover that in less than half a minute! A round-trip would take twice as long, or about one minute.

Le Jingyi of China set a women's world record for the 50-meter freestyle. She finished the race in an amazing 24.51 seconds!

The 400-meter freestyle is four round-trips in the pool. About how long does it take? Look at Janet Evans's numbers from the 1988 Olympics. Pay close attention to the "splits." (A *split* is a time for one segment of a race. One split is usually one round-trip, or 100 meters.)

Meters	Elapsed Time (seconds)	Split (seconds)
100	59.99	59.99
200	122.14	62.15
300	183.40	61.26
400	243.85	60.45

Each round-trip took Janet about one minute. Three of the four splits are just over a minute. So you can *estimate* that Janet's world-record time is about four minutes. Or you can add up the times and learn that her record is exactly 4:03.85 (4 minutes and 3.85 seconds).

Use what you know about Janet's times to answer these questions: About how many minutes is Janet's world record in the 800 meters? What is her world-record time in the 1,500 meters? *(Answers on pages 62-64.)*

DIVE INTO DIVING

Let's say you want to impress your friends. Would you do an easy dive? Or would you try a tough dive and risk goofing it up?

In diving, it's important for dives to look good. But it's also important for divers to take risks.

Men and women compete separately, but they perform the same dives and are scored the same way.

A panel of five to seven judges gives each dive a score. There are seven judges in the Olympics. The scores range from 0 (a total bomb) to 10 (a perfect dive).

Let's say you're a diver. Here's a sample set of scores for you:

6.7 7.5 7.1 6.6 7.2 7.6 7.0

The highest score and the lowest score are always tossed out. The rest are added together. In the example above, your total is 35.5 (the 7.6 and 6.6 scores were tossed

GREG LOUGANIS

out). That total is then multiplied by .6 or ⅗:

35.5 x .6 = 21.3 (judges' score)

But that's not all! To get a diver's *final* score, the judges' score is multiplied by a "degree of difficulty" rating. That ranges from 1.1 to 3.5 or even higher. The harder the dive, the higher the number. An easy dive gets a 1.2. A hard dive can earn a 3.5 or more. Say you do a dive with a difficulty rating of 2.0. What's your total score? Use the sample scores from page 43.

In 1983, Greg Louganis of the U.S. set the record for the highest score on the springboard: 755.49. That's almost 69 points per dive! Greg won four gold medals and one silver in Olympic competition. He also won five world championships! He is the greatest American diver of alltime.

DO SOME SPLITS

In 1994, American Tom Dolan set the world record in the 400-meter individual medley. His times for each 100-meter split looked like this:

> 58.28 seconds (butterfly)
> 64.62 seconds (backstroke)
> 71.76 seconds (breaststroke)
> 57.64 seconds (freestyle)

1. What was Tom's total record-setting time in minutes and seconds? _____

2. Which two splits did Tom swim the fastest? _____

(Answers on pages 62–64.)

CHAPTER 6

HOCKEY

What can burn up the ice at speeds of over 100 miles per hour? No, not a Zamboni. A hockey puck! Especially a puck shot by Wayne Gretzky. He is one of the game's greatest players. In fact, his nickname is "The Great One."

In his career, Wayne has netted some of the greatest stats in history. How does he stack up to other greats of the game? The answer is in the numbers.

SETTLING THE SCORE

When is a scorer a *great* goal-scorer? When he scores goal number 500. By the end of the 1995–96 season, Wayne Gretzky had scored 883 goals in his pro career (as a member of the World Hockey League and the National Hockey League). Hall-of-Famer Gordie Howe scored 975 goals in his career. They don't call him "Mr. Hockey" for nothing! So was Gordie the better scorer? Or does Wayne rule?

Gordie had more total goals. But Wayne has scored at a faster rate. Gordie scored his 500th NHL goal after playing 1,045 games. Wayne did it in almost half that time — 575 games. No other player has come close to doing it that fast. Sounds like Wayne's the better scorer.

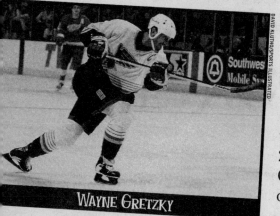

DAVID KLUTHO/SPORTS ILLUSTRATED

WAYNE GRETZKY

Not so fast. Gordie had the longest career of *any* NHL player. He spent 26 seasons in the league! Wayne Gretzky would have to play to the year 2004 to hit 26 seasons. So, does Gordie Howe come out on top?

To figure who was the better scorer, you have to do more than compare raw numbers, such as total goals. You have to compare averages. In this case, compare the average number of goals each player scored per game. That stat is called "goals per game." How do you figure points per game?

First, divide the total number of goals scored by the number of games played. Then, round your answer to the nearest hundredth.

Gordie:
  500 goals ÷ 1,045 games = .48 goals per game
Wayne:
  500 goals ÷ 575 games = .87 goals per game

Gordie's goals-per-game average was .48 — about half a goal per game. Wayne's .87 is much closer to one goal per game. So it seems fair to say that the Great One is a better scorer than Mr. Hockey.

SCORING POINTS

Goals scored aren't the only measure of a hockey player's greatness. *Assists* count too. (A player gets an assist by making a pass that leads to a goal. Say you pass the puck to the Flyers' Eric Lindros. He shoots. He scores! Eric gets the goal, and you get an assist.)

A player's point total is a combination of goals and assists:

goals + assists = points

In personal stats, goals and assists count equally. Players who pass the puck to a goal scorer get just as much credit as the scorer: 1 point apiece. Of course, the scorer gets 1 point plus most of the glory. You can't put a number on glory.

Say you have a fantastic game. You score three goals and get three assists. What's your point total for the

WACKY FACT

When a player scores three goals in a game, it's called a hat trick. It's a tough stunt to pull off, but not impossible. Wayne Gretzky has 49 of them!

By the end of each NHL season, a handful of players have scored 4 goals in a game. One or two have scored 5 goals. Not since 1976 has a player (Darryl Sittler of the Toronto Maple Leafs) scored 6 goals. And 7 goals? Travel back to 1920. Joe Malone of the Québec Bulldogs is the only player in NHL history to do it!

night? Six points (3 + 3 = 6).

When it comes to all-time leaders in points, goals, and assists, it's Wayne Gretzky all the way. After the 1995–96 season, he was first in career NHL goals (837), assists (1,771), and points (2,608).

GOAL FOR IT

Goaltenders' stats aren't about scoring. They're about *not* scoring! Like a baseball pitcher hoping to give up very few hits, a goalie's aim is to give up very few goals. A shutout — no goals in a game — is even better. Like pitchers, goalies keep track of games won and lost.

Terry Sawchuck is the current victory king, with 447 career wins. (He played from 1949 to 1970.) In the 1973–74 season, Bernie Parent set the record for the most wins in one season. The Philadelphia Flyer goalie won a whopping 47 games that year.

Goalie Manon Rheaume (*ma-NO ray-OME*) was the first woman to play in an NHL game. In 1992, she tended goal in an exhibition game: the Tampa Bay Lightning

WACKY FACT

The penalty box is sometimes called the "sin bin." Dave Williams spent so much time there, it was like a second home to him! Dave holds the NHL record for most career penalty minutes: 4,421 (including post-season games). If Dave had served all of of his penalties in a row, he would have been in the box for more than three days!

WACKY FACT

A Zamboni is a machine that drives over bumpy ice and leaves nice, smooth ice behind. Before it was invented, it would take a crew of five men about 90 minutes to resurface a rink. A single Zamboni can do the job in about 15 minutes!

versus the St. Louis Blues.

Over the next three seasons, Manon played for five minor league teams. In 1993–94 she had a record of five wins and one loss with the East Coast Hockey League. Her numbers:

- 8 games played (6 as the goalie of record)
- 5 games won
- 1 game lost (in overtime)
- 385 minutes played
- 25 goals against

Manon's won-loss record is solid. But how else can you measure a goalie's success? Once again, averages are the way to go.

In a goalie's case, the average is called a "goals against average" (GAA). It works a lot like a pitcher's earned run average. The GAA is the number of goals given up versus the amount of time played. The longer a goalie plays without giving up goals, the lower the average. The lower the average, the better.

Back to Manon. Here's how to figure her goals against average:

1. Multiply the "goals against" by 60 (the number of minutes in a regulation game):

25 goals against x 60 minutes = 1,500

2. Divide the answer by the number of minutes played:

1,500 minutes ÷ 385 minutes = 3.896

3. Round to two decimal places: **3.90**

It's harder to maintain a low average when you play a lot of games. Goalie Chris Osgood helped the Detroit Red Wings win a record number of games in the 1995–96 season. Chris allowed 106 goals in 2,933 minutes of playing time. What's his GAA?   *(Answers on pages 62-64.)*

   1. 106 x 60 = _____
   2. _____ ÷ 2,933 = _____
   3. GAA = _____

FAST FACT

WHOOMP— there it is! You scored! How fast could you or one of your teammates score another goal? Several NHL teams have shot back-to-back goals within 4 seconds of play! The Calgary Flames were the last to accomplish that amazing feat, in 1989.

BY THE NUMBERS

Can you identify this
"super" Pittsburgh Penguin
by his numbers?

BIRTHDATE: 10/5/65
JERSEY NUMBER: 66
HEIGHT: 6 feet, 4 inches
WEIGHT: 220 pounds
CLAIM TO FAME: .842 goals
per game average

(Answers on
pages 62–64.)

SHORTCUTS

Hockey is a speedy sport. So don't waste a minute –
take a quick timeout to brush up on abbreviations:

A = Assists
G = Goals
GA = Goals against (goals that other teams score)
GF = Goals for (goals that your team scores)
GP = Games played
Min. = Minutes played
Pts. = Points

BUFFALO BONANZA

In 1981 the Buffalo Sabres scored 9 goals in one period against the Toronto Maple Leafs. A period is 20 minutes long. So how many minutes per goal did the Sabres
average? To find out, divide 20 by 9:

20 ÷ 9 = 2.22 minutes per goal

REIGN OF THE ROY

CRAIG MELVIN/SPORTS CHROME EAST/WEST

PATRICK ROY

Colorado Avalanche goalie Patrick Roy (pronounced *WAH*) was a hero of the 1996 Stanley Cup playoffs. Ten years earlier, as a Montreal Canadien, Patrick tended goal in the 1986 Stanley Cup playoffs. For which team did Patrick have a better goals against average? *(Answers on pages 62–64.)*

	Minutes	GA	GAA
1986	1,218	39	_____
1996	1,454	51	_____

WAY, NO WAY

Do you know a bogus stat when you see one? Read the list below and say whether each feat is possible ("Way") or impossible ("No way") in the NHL.

Statistic	Way/No Way
1. 62 wins in a season for a team	_____
2. 5 goals in a period	_____
3. A goal scored .1 second into the game	_____
4. A 412-minute game	_____
5. 139 points in a season for a goalie	_____
6. 2 Stanley Cup titles for an individual	_____

(Answers on pages 62–64.)

CHAPTER 7

TRACK AND FIELD

According to the world famous scientist Albert Einstein, the faster we go, the smaller we get. We're not really sure what Albert meant by that, but we'll take his word for it. We do know that getting smaller is not the goal of track and field. But the sport *does* use lots of of itty-bitty numbers to measure speed and distance.

TIME FLIES

On July 6, 1994, American sprinter Leroy Burrell became the world's fastest human. He ran the 100-meter dash in 9.85 seconds. His time was just one-hundredth (.01) of a second faster than the previous record. How fast is a hundredth of a second? You can't say "I win" that fast! Here's how Leroy's winning number breaks down:

9.85 seconds = 9 seconds + $\frac{8}{10}$ second + $\frac{5}{100}$ second

Mary Decker Slaney holds the American record for a

longer race — the 3,000 meters. Her record is 8:25.83. The colon separates minutes from seconds. Minutes are to the left of the colon, and seconds are to the right.

The 3,000-meter race is slower than the 100-meter race, but hundredths of a second still count:

$$8:25.83 =$$
8 minutes + 25 seconds + 8/10 second + 3/100 second

Joan Benoit's American record for the marathon is 2:21:21. This time there are *two* colons. Why? Because the marathon is one *very* long race — more than 26 miles! The first colon (the one farthest to the left) separates hours and minutes. The second colon separates minutes and seconds. Fractions of a second no longer matter:

$$2:21:21 =$$
2 hours + 21 minutes + 21 seconds

WACKY FACT

In 1968 Bob Beamon did something that seemed impossible. He long-jumped 29 feet 2½ inches. Bob shattered the world record by almost two feet.

No one believed a person could jump that far. And no one did it again until Mike Powell came along. Mike was 4 years old in 1968. In 1991, he jumped two inches farther than Bob Beamon had jumped!

UP, UP, AND AWAY

The long jump, triple jump, javelin, shot put, hammer, and discus all have one thing in common: distance. The longer the distance, the better.

High jump and pole vault are all about altitude, or height. Take a look at a standard ceiling. It's about eight feet high. That's how high the bar is set for high jumper Javier Sotomayor. He set the record of 8' ½" in 1993. Javier is the only human being ever to jump higher than eight feet.

Now picture a two-story house. Most pole vaulters could fly over it! Sergei Bubka of Ukraine holds the world record of 20 feet 1¾ inches.

HITTING THE WALL

The Olympic motto is FASTER, HIGHER, STRONGER. Since the first modern games, in 1896, athletes have lived up to this ideal. In 1896, American Robert Garrett took the gold in the shot put with a toss of 36 feet 9¾ inches. From the goal line of a football field, that's just past the 12-yard line.

BOB BEAMON

Today's Olympians can heave that 16-pound ball 72 feet — or to the 24-yard line. If things continue at this pace, the winning distance will be *144 feet* in about a hundred years! Do you think that's possible?

OLYMPIC GOLD, THEN AND NOW

Event	Winning Distance	
	1896	1992
Men's Triple Jump	44' 11½"	59' 7½"
Men's High Jump	5' 11¼"	7' 8¼"
Men's Pole Vault	10' 10"	19' ½"
Men's Discus	95' 7½"	213' 7¾"
Women's Javelin	143' 4"	224' 2½"
Women's Long Jump	18' 8¼"	23' 5¼"
Women's High Jump	5' 2½"	6' 7½"
Women's Shot Put	45' 1½"	69' 1¼"

GOLD DIGGERS

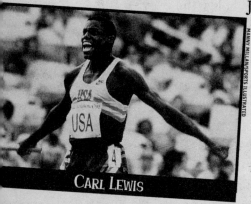

CARL LEWIS

Jesse Owens was an Olympic gold digger in the 1930s. Carl Lewis mined for Olympic gold in the 1980s and 1990s.

Can you tell who's who by their stats? One set belongs to Carl. The other list of accomplishments belongs to Jesse.

A. TRACK STAR: _____
- won four gold medals in one Olympics
- set world records in the 200 meters, long jump, and 400-meter relay
- long-jump record stood for 25 years
- born in Alabama and grew up in Ohio

B. TRACK STAR: _____

- won four gold medals in one Olympics
- won the long jump three straight Olympics
- set a world record in the 100-meter dash
- has won eight gold medals and one silver medal at three Olympics

IF YOU HAD A HAMMER

Take a ball, a spear, a disk, and a hammer. Which one could you throw the farthest? Could you come close to these record distances? Probably not. But here's something you *can* do: Match each world-record distance with one of the field events listed below.

Event	Men's World Record
1. Discus	A. 313 feet 10 inches
2. Hammer	B. 75 feet 10¼
3. Shot put	C. 243 feet
4. Javelin	D. 284 feet 7 inches

WACKY FACT

On May 25, 1935, track legend Jesse Owens set five world records and tied a sixth. And he did it in less than one hour! He ran 100 yards in 9.4 seconds, tying the world record. He long-jumped 26 feet 8¼ inches. Then he ran 220 yards in 20.3 seconds and the 220-yard hurdles in 22.6 seconds. Jesse also set world records in the 200 meters and 200-meter hurdles.

BEASTIE FEATS

How fast can a human swim without flippers or any other help? This graph shows the top speeds of swimmers, runners, skaters, and multi-legged beasts. Say they all competed in one crazy race. Can you pick the winner?

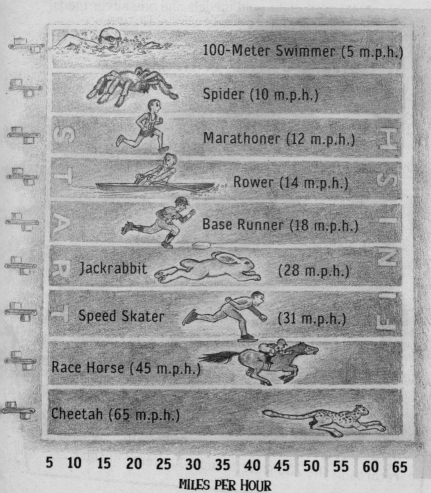

100-Meter Swimmer (5 m.p.h.)

Spider (10 m.p.h.)

Marathoner (12 m.p.h.)

Rower (14 m.p.h.)

Base Runner (18 m.p.h.)

Jackrabbit (28 m.p.h.)

Speed Skater (31 m.p.h.)

Race Horse (45 m.p.h.)

Cheetah (65 m.p.h.)

5 10 15 20 25 30 35 40 45 50 55 60 65

MILES PER HOUR

CHAPTER 8

ALL-STAR ROUNDUP

Okay, you've read the book. But are you a true sports math maniac? Take a shot at this all-star quiz to find out!

1. If your batting average is .300, it means
   (a) you are perfect.
   (b) you get three hits in every 10 at-bats.
   (c) you should switch to golf.

2. FOUL! One of these stats does not belong on a basketball court. Which one should be bounced out?
   (a) Points per game
   (b) Rebounds per game
   (c) Goals against average

3. Atlanta Brave pitcher Greg Maddux had a .905 winning percentage in 1995. Was that a good winning percentage or a bad one?

4. Paul Coffey is a hockey superstar. But what if someone told you that the Detroit Red Wing defender scored 48 goals in one season. What would a true sports math maniac say in response?

(a) "That's impossible — defenders don't score."

(b) "It sounds like a scoring record for a defenseman."

(c) "He stinks."

5. The Pfeffer brothers, Fred and Big Jeff, played baseball in the early part of this century. Fred retired with a .255 batting average. Big Jeff had 66 hits in 323 at-bats. Which Pfeffer hit better?

(a) Fred

(b) Big Jeff

(c) Neither — they were equally bad.

6. **True or false:** It's possible to have a 109-yard kick-off return in a football game.

7. You have invented a sport — surfboard-volleyball! How many countries must play it before it can be an Olympic sport for women? At least . . .

(a) 100 countries. (b) 1 country. (c) 35 countries.

8. In swimming, a split is
   (a) a time for a half-segment of a race.
   (b) a time for one segment of a race.
   (c) a tasty ice cream sundae with bananas.

9. **True or false:** A spider can beat a top human marathon runner in a race.

10. Jersey numbers often tell which position a football player plays. Ends usually wear 80–89; tackles, 70–79; guards, 60–69; centers, 50–59; backs, 10–49. Barry Sanders plays the position with the greatest amount of numbers to chose from. *Which position does he play?*

ANSWERS

CHAPTER 1

WHAT'S A BATTING AVERAGE? *(Page 8):*
1. Edgar Martinez .356 (his average is the best of the bunch); **2.** Chili Davis .318; **3.** Albert Belle .317

ERA: PITCHERS GIVE IT UP *(Page 10):* .294

BY THE NUMBERS *(Page 10):* Cal Ripken, Junior.

GOOD, THE BAD, AND AVERAGE *(Page 11):*
1. If a batter gets 9 RBI's in a season, he had a bad year. But 9 RBI's in *a game* is a different story. That's great!
2. .590 is a *good* win-loss percentage for a season.

THINK FAST!*(Page 12):* John Neves wore a backwards 7 because his last name is seven spelled backwards!

ABOVE AVERAGE *(Page 12):* .406

BELOW AVERAGE *(Page 13):* .301

BY THE NUMBERS *(Page 13):* The player is Joe DiMaggio. In 1941, he hit safely in 56 straight games.

MYSTERY PITCHER *(Page 13):* The mystery pitcher is Greg Maddux; his ERA, rounded to two decimal places, is 1.64.

LITTLE LEAGUE *(Page 14):* Taiwan is tops with 15 championships.

NUMBER HALL OF FAME *(Page 15):* **1.** F (Hack Wilson); **2.** G (Hank Aaron); **3.** E (Cy Young); **4.** B(Roger Maris); **5.** C (Pete Rose); **6.** A (Hank Aaron); **7.** H (Nolan Ryan). **8.** G (Joe DiMaggio)

WELCOME TO THE CLUB? *(Page 16):* Al Kaline's homer total was 399. It's one run short of the 400-3,000 club!

WHERE THE SON SHINES *(Page 15):* **1.** Batting average; **2.** Ken Griffey, Senior; **3.** Answers will vary; **4.** Answers will vary; **5.** Compare *averages*

CHAPTER 2

BE LIKE MIKE *(Page 19):* **1986–87:** 37.1; **1987–88:** 35.0; **1988–89:** 32.5; **1990–91:** 31.5; *Michael had the highest average in 1986–87.*

BY THE NUMBERS *(Page 20):* Michael Jordan (He led the Chicago Bulls to three championships in a row from 1991–1993.)

BY THE NUMBERS *(Page 23):* Kareem Abdul-Jabbar (He played a record 20 seasons in the NBA.)

GIVE THEM A HAND *(Page 24):* Through the 1995-96 season, John Stockton had averaged 11.54 assists per game. Magic Johnson averaged 11.19 per game.

RODMAN'S REBOUNDS *(Page 24):* 17.27

FOUL CALL *(Page 24):* Reggie's the best at .877 (87.7 percent). Scottie is second with .687 (68.7 percent). Shaq is third with .545 (54.5 percent).

CHAPTER 3

POWERFUL PELÉ *(Page 29):* .95 goals per game

CHAPTER 4

BY THE NUMBERS *(Page 35):* Chicago Bear Hall-of-Famer Walter Payton. (He gained 16,726 yards on 3,838 carries and 4,537 yards on 492 receptions!)

TOUCHDOWN! *(Page 36):* Emmitt averaged 1.56 touchdowns per game. Jerry's average is better.

BY THE NUMBERS *(Page 36):* Dallas Cowboy Troy Aikman. (He led his team to three Super Bowl victories.)

ANY WHICH WAY IT'S 12 *(Page 38):* There are many different ways to score 12 points in a football game. Here are a few: 2 touchdowns (6 + 6); 4 field goals (3 + 3 + 3 + 3); 6 safeties (2 + 2 + 2 + 2 + 2 + 2); 1 touchdown, 2 field goals (6 + 3 + 3); 2 field goals, 3 safeties (3 + 3 + 2 + 2 + 2)

JUST PASSING BY *(Page 38):* 3

WHAT'S THE CATCH? *(Page 38):* 7.6

JIM VS. WALTER *(Page 38):* Jim wins. (Multiply 4 years by 1,368 yards per year to get 5,472 extra yards. Add the extra yards to Jim's 12,312 to get 17,784 yards.)

ALMOST PERFECT *(Page 39):* 80.43 percent (divide 366 by 455)

TACKLING TERROR *(Page 39):* 121.5 tackles per year

OH, BROTHER *(Page 40):* Sterling Sharpe: 11.9; Shannon Sharpe: 11.6; Rocket Ismail: 15.1; Qadry Ismail: 15.5. Both Ismails come out ahead of the Sharpes.

CHAPTER 5

JUST A MINUTE *(Page 42):* About 8 minutes (8:16.22) in the 800 meters; about 15 minutes (15:52.10) in the 1500 meters.

DIVE INTO DIVING *(Page 43):* Your total score is 42.6 (Multiply the judges' score by the degree of difficulty.)

DO SOME SPLITS *(Page 44):* **(1)** 4 minutes, 12.30 seconds; **(2)** The freestyle and the butterfly

CHAPTER 6

GOAL FOR IT *(Page 50):*
1. 106 x 60 = *6,360;* 2. *6,360* ÷ 2,933 = *2.168;* 3. GAA = *2.17*

BY THE NUMBERS *(Page 51):* Mario Lemieux

REIGN OF THE ROY *(Page 52):* 1986 GAA = 1.92; 1996 GAA = 2.10 (Patrick was better in 1986.)

WAY, NO WAY *(Page 52):* **1.** Way; **2.** Way; **3.** No way (No human being can shoot that fast.); **4.** No way (That would be more than 20 periods of play!); **5.** No way (*One* goal in a season is good for a goalie!); **6.** Way

CHAPTER 7

GOLD DIGGERS *(Page 56):* Track star A is Jesse Owens; B is Carl Lewis.

IF YOU HAD A HAMMER *(Page 57):* **1.** C; **2.** D; **3.** B; **4.** A

BEASTIE FEATS *(Page 58):* The cheetah would win.

CHAPTER 8

ALL-STAR ROUNDUP *(Pages 59–61):*
(1) b; **(2)** c; **(3)** .905 is a *great* winning percentage;
(4) b (It *is* a record for a defenseman!); **(5)** a;
(6) True; **(7)** c; **(8)** b;
(9) False; **(10)** Barry Sanders is a *back* (a running back) His jersey number is 20.

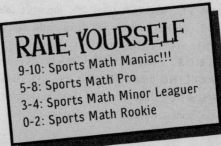

RATE YOURSELF

9-10: Sports Math Maniac!!!
5-8: Sports Math Pro
3-4: Sports Math Minor Leaguer
0-2: Sports Math Rookie